Magnificent MIND

Uncover Your Psychological Well Being So You Can Live in Heaven While on Earth

Jan Christenson

Magnificent Mind
Copyright © 2020 by Jan Christenson

All rights reserved. No part of this publication
may be reproduced, distributed, or transmitted
in any form or by any means, including
photocopying, recording, or other electronic
or mechanical methods, without the prior
written permission of the author, except
in the case of brief quotations embodied
in critical reviews and certain other non-
commercial uses permitted by copyright law.

tellwell

Tellwell Talent
www.tellwell.ca

ISBN
978-0-2288-2206-6 (Hardcover)
978-0-2288-2205-9 (Paperback)
978-0-2288-2207-3 (eBook)

This book is dedicated to my two daughters, Jessie and Kerri. I hope that it will help you find inner peace and contentment. If it can help others live a more peaceful life, I would be forever grateful.

TABLE OF CONTENTS

INTRODUCTION 5

CHAPTER 1: Understanding the Psychology of Humans 9

CHAPTER 2: History of Psychology 18

CHAPTER 3: The Three Principles of Mind, Consciousness, and Thought 31

CHAPTER 4: Mind 44

CHAPTER 5: Consciousness 53

CHAPTER 6: Thought 64

CHAPTER 7: Science that Relates to Consciousness, Mind, and Thought 70

CHAPTER 8: Finding your Wisdom 75

CHAPTER 9: The Self 78

CHAPTER 10: Capabilities of the Mind 82

CHAPTER 11: Love 86

ACKNOWLEDGEMENTS 91

WORKS CITED 95

How the three principles helped me write a book when I felt it was impossible, for me, to write a book

I thought that writing a book was for those people who were smarter than me, who were more educated than me, and who had more interesting stories to tell. It turns out that when I embraced the three principles of understanding, I could see for myself that no one is wiser than me and no one is wiser than you either. This inner wisdom that we all have allows me and also you to do anything that we truly want to do.

By truly accepting this truth that anything is possible, I had a chance to throw the doors wide open and just see what I might want to do in this precious life of mine. As I saw that we are all energy in form and formlessness, it made sense to me that on a small scale I was the same energy that everything is made of. Everything is made of energy and energy forms to create mass. On the bigger and biggest scale, I am the same energy that makes up the entire universe.

When you realize that you and the whole universe are flowing together, you know that this divine energy that is out there is also inside of you. This understanding gave me a whole new view of myself and others. It occurred to me that I needed to be true to myself and become as magnificent in my life as I felt and knew I was inwardly in spirit or energy. While I'm in this form, it feels like bringing this energy out to play. With the form and the formless combined, the possibilities are endless.

I felt strongly that the experiences shown to me by magnificent universal wisdom needed to change my life and be shared with others so that they too could move on to live their most rich lives. The rich life I am speaking of is one of tapping into your inner energy which exudes a well-being that is peaceful, loving, and free of any fear.

I was showered with this peaceful, loving energy when I took a dip into what seemed to me to maybe be death, and at that time it freed me of my body, my mass, and my being here on Earth. This experience showed me the place where my spirit goes when I leave my body behind. I almost stayed there because I was so free to soar and flow endlessly in that energy. I felt the complete contentment of the energy of love and peace that is our spirit. Then, quite freely, I chose to return to my place on Earth in energy and mass and, yes, love and contentment too.

The energy that flows in us when we are humans is our ride to freedom to be and do anything, while in this body form, that we so choose to do. There is nothing to fear in this life. Not even in death, as I have seen, is there any fear. This death that we speak of and often fear is just a shift in energy where we are no longer contained in our body. Our spirit then takes us to a place of bliss. This is not so bad; in fact, it is splendidly magnificent.

I had to learn to take myself much less seriously after this experience. This brought me to the realization that I am totally free to let go of any thoughts that I don't feel are in alignment with the truly divine being that I am, as we all are.

I no longer had to be stuck in the idea that I was a shy introvert who had little to say to the world. This thinking was not true; it was limited to a square box type of thinking that led to a narrow path of existence for me. My new truth is that I am completely free to be who I choose to be from moment to moment in this present life of mine. No longer does anyone else get to say who or what I am.

People are free to say what they like about me, but what they have to say is of no concern and has no consequences for me. It is a whole new inside-out thinking that brings me to my own truths in which a very desirable existence is to be had. I have no more opinions and judgments that I meet people with.

Then, being totally human, I may have the experience of completely forgetting this newfound existence and taking my thinking to lack of confidence and lack of inner peace until I remember the human experience of thought is all just made up and then lived out. Recalling this takes me back to the peaceful, nice feeling of just living in the moment with nothing to fear, nothing to worry about. Simply enjoy the moment and do the things that need to be done, one thing at a time. Enjoy each moment. No real agenda is needed as the energy just flows through me, and my life is created while in this flow.

In this flow I have written a book to try to share this understanding of mind, consciousness, and thought. These principles have brought me to such a lovely life of contentment and unconditional love for all others. It has occurred to me that I want to share this knowledge with anyone who might like to improve some or all of their life experiences.

INTRODUCTION

What is the purpose of life? What does a successful life look like, or what does it not look like? In our world today most people live with tremendous stress and they are just hanging on by a thread. They try to look calm and cool on the outside, yet they are in turmoil on the inside. Or you will find people who are just plain angry, usually because they have a lot of fear inside of them.

A stressful life can make you very angry or hopeless. To cope with the stress, people will often look for something to lift them out of these feelings of worry and stress. They may often turn to abuse of alcohol, food, or drugs as a quick fix to the stress and possibly depression they might be feeling. What if I could show you a way to relieve the depression and let go of the addictions? Would you be interested in trying a really helpful way of dealing with these problems?

I can show you how to understand your thinking. This might give you what you need to know in order to free yourself of mental health issues or the quick-fix methods of addictions. This can lead to a successful life which I think is happiness, contentment, and love. If this sounds like what you need right now, then this book is for you.

I have lived with very high stress in my life, which led to anger, depression, and addiction. This is a horrible way to live. I felt unhappy and desperately needed to change something for my family and for myself. When you really need things in life and are ready for change, the right people and the right things just seem to start showing up if you pay attention.

There are no coincidences in life and everything happens for a reason. The fact that you are reading this book is a very good sign that it may be your time to learn of some new ways to live a fulfilling life. It is not only possible but also quite easy for you to find inner peace, contentment, and love for yourself and others.

I have arrived at a place inside of myself that is honestly heaven on Earth. There are still problems that arise, but they just don't have any stress or inner turmoil arriving with them. I can move through difficulties with new knowledge that just carries me through with ease and grace.

Ease and grace are much more preferable conditions compared to my old way of hellish confusion and conflict. You can have these changes too if you open your mind and thought to a new way in life. No one really wants to live in pain and suffering.

If you don't learn a new way well, you may just live many more years with unnecessary pain and suffering. We all have access to a divine inner wisdom that is ever present and waiting for us to discover. This inner wisdom in you and me is always healthy, no matter what we have lived through.

You are never broken; there is always this healthy spark inside of you. We are all born with a healthy psychological state inside, it is just a matter of getting back to it.

This inner health and wisdom comprises your magnificent mind. Understanding and living in this knowing can take you home to who you really are, and then the possibilities for you are unlimited. This wisdom will give you answers to any of your questions about yourself and your life that you may have. Settling into your peaceful mind will give you gifts that you cannot possibly know until you experience them. I hope you enjoy your journey through this book.

CHAPTER 1

Understanding the Psychology of Humans

"With hope and faith as beacons, anything can happen."

Quotation from *The Missing Link* by Sydney Banks

We all experience our life through the thoughts we have going on inside of us. One thought at a time, we create our reality and then we live in that reality. That's just how powerful our thoughts are; they create our life.

If your thoughts are, "I am so shy that I don't think people even notice that I am here," you might then feel kind of sad or lonely. When you are around people, you might then be very quiet. This can lead to people not really noticing you, because you are so quiet.

Whatever we are thinking about ourselves or the events unfolding around us, here is what happens: we have a thought, this is usually followed by an emotional response, and then a behaviour of some sort will often occur. This is just how we humans work inside: a thought followed by an emotion and then a behaviour.

So if we could all just think, "What a great, divine being I am," then the emotion could be one of pure joy and love, and the behaviour to follow might be to treat others with love and respect. Wow, that sounds so easy, and it sounds like such a beautiful state to live out our time here on Earth. Let's just come back to the reality that most people live in. We live in a time and place where people are feeling frustrated, angry, and lonely.

Even when we do our best to live life as a good human being, inside there can be thoughts of never being enough, never doing enough. We can be so hard on ourselves. We can have one face that we show to our family. We have different ways of being that we show to our co-workers, to our friends, and to the world in general. If this is your experience of life, then you know it can get very confusing.

It can be hard to figure out who you really are and how you can present this self comfortably in all of the different places in your life. There is a way to do this, though. If you learn to just live in the moment and be really present to looking at and listening to what is around you, then you can engage with present life as it unfolds and not live by and through your inner chatter. By being curious and looking for the good in yourself and others, you can become interested in your life and become quiet inside of your head.

The opposite of inner quiet is noisy chatter in your head. We all have it going on: that non-stop ticker tape of thought after thought after thought running through our head. I know that if I think of problems of the past, problems of the present, and then problems of the future, it can be overwhelming. I know that during these times I would feel that I couldn't continue living like I was. For years I thought that I had to in some way fix myself, that I was broken.

There is simply no truth to these thoughts. I am not broken, and the good news is that you are not broken either. We are all not broken, we are fine. I have learned that when you have a lot of inner chatter and disturbing thoughts of any kind going on inside of you, there is a solution. You simply have to understand how thoughts work, and then you can break out of the vicious cycle of pain and suffering that accompanies unhealthy thoughts. You simply have to let go of the thoughts that are not working in a way that makes your life better. If it's not that easy to just stop the thoughts, then at least stop believing them. You might wonder, "Can it be that easy?"

Yes, it can be that easy. It might just take one or two new healthy thoughts to bring joy into your life and awaken your healthy, spirited self. If you can open your mind to a new way of paying no attention to your unhealthy thinking, then you can change all that holds you back from becoming all that you were meant to be.

I have learned about thoughts through the three principles of mind, consciousness, and thought. These principles have been well articulated by Sydney Banks in his books and recorded conversations.

When I read books written by Sydney Banks and listened to his recorded conversations from years gone by, it stirred a feeling of well-being inside of me that was not totally unfamiliar to me. It took me a bit of time to understand the feeling.

I came to understand this inner feeling as my inner innate health that had always been there. I developed a thirst for understanding what these principles were all about. As I read more, I felt more peace and love for myself and others.

I want to welcome you to the possibility of finding a whole new way of living with joy in your heart, feeling love for life, and experiencing this peacefulness that you have inside. It became very clear to me that this feeling inside of me had always been there; I just hadn't accessed it for a long time. You also have always had this healthy peaceful state inside; it is just a matter of you getting back to it.

We are born with a perfectly healthy state of psychological well-being inside of us. Day by day we grow and learn and have unhealthy thoughts that cover this state of well-being. As we grow, we learn opinions, beliefs, and judgments. As we are taught these beliefs and opinions, they seem to become truths that chatter in our heads. With ideas of how we should be, we then learn to compare ourselves to others. As we make these self-comparisons, we feel less and less of all of the greatness we have inside. We become open to all the thoughts of not being enough and not knowing enough. We don't feel very capable of anything.

We are free at any time to untangle this web of untrue beliefs that we have developed about ourselves. I have found it very helpful to drop away the beliefs and judgments of not being enough. When you simply let the thoughts of being inadequate fall away, you will find that you have a whole new abundance of energy to put into your life.

This newfound energy can be used to reignite the greatness that is within you. This dropping away of beliefs and judgments of self and others makes room for acceptance and love for anyone that crosses your path. You simply relax into each moment of your life, knowing you have an inner space that is healthy and whole at all times.

This knowing of an inner health has come through living life one moment at a time, with no judgment of self or others, and acknowledging the clear, inner knowledge that guides me and keeps me safe at all times. Learning about the three principles has helped me to see these truths, and this process has changed my life completely. The way that I relate to people has changed, the way I treat myself has changed, and the way I see life has changed.

Worrying was a way of life for me: I worried about everything and everyone. I worried if things seemed bad, I worried if things seemed good, and if I wasn't worrying I knew there must be something I should be worrying about. I thought that to live was to worry. It turns out that I was misguided in this belief, as I was also misguided in so many beliefs and judgments that I had learned. In my head, I had just thought that they were true.

I have learned what thoughts really are and how I can make use of this knowledge to create the life I want and deserve to live. You see, our thoughts are just thoughts and they don't have to mean anything. You don't have to pay attention to your thoughts, and you should never be afraid of them. Just because you think something does not mean you have to act on it. Most of the time, a thought does not require an action.

You can let go of any thought that you choose. There are many thoughts that, if you allowed them to stay in your head, would lead you to becoming healthy. When you let the unhealthy thoughts go, life takes on a delightful easy flow accompanied by a really special feeling.

This inner feeling is a gentle feeling, sort of like butterflies in your stomach. You just feel connected, a real sense of belonging, a feeling of being a part of all that is in you and fully connected to all that is around you. Learning and feeling this has left me with a clear sense of how very much I am just fine. I know that the thoughts and decisions in my life have led me here to this present moment, and it is perfect. I belong right here, right now. This can become your truth too.

This is your place and your time to learn a new way of not just existing but truly experiencing your life as a blessing to be enjoyed and cherished by you. There is a perfectly healthy psychological state inside of you just waiting to be discovered. Don't wait another moment: dive in and discover your existence as the divine gift it is meant to be. Let the waves of change wash over you and become all that you were meant to be. You will learn your path to a life that can feel like heaven on Earth.

Some people can live in the most lavish conditions and they are utterly miserable, and others can live with pretty much nothing and they are as happy as they can possibly be. What is it that allows some people to be so happy, no matter their circumstances?

I think it is safe to say that money and possessions are not the difference-maker in happiness. Some people can have a background of little to no problems or suffering and they are hateful and spiteful, while others may have had the most horrendous of things happen to and around them and they remain compassionate and loving. So what creates such a wide range of individual differences in people's worlds?

Since we can only ever experience the world from our own perspective, we create our own reality one thought at a time. We, as humans, all work the same, and how we think is the same process for all of us. It is just that what we think and what we do with that thinking differs from one person to another, and so we create these different realities that become our lives.

I spent a lot of time in my life trying to become mentally healthier by reading self-development books. I went to university, achieved a B.A. in psychology, and I sought help in therapy. I tried talking, I tried behaviour modification, I tried meditating, I tried medication, I tried counselling, I tried yoga, I tried reflexology. If you can name it, I have probably tried it. Some of these techniques and treatments helped, but needing fixing remained the focus. Then I came across the three principles of mind, consciousness, and thought, and my life changed for the better almost immediately. With this understanding, the realization set in that no one is broken, no one needs to be fixed, and there really is very little to do to be healthy psychologically.

CHAPTER 2

History of Psychology

"Achieving mental stability is a matter of finding healthy thoughts from moment to moment."

Quotation from *The Missing Link* by Sydney Banks

When I learned about Sydney Banks and his very different approach to viewing mental wellness, I was able to make sense of a lot of otherwise mysterious human behaviour. The three principles gave me hope, love, and a peaceful mind. But, before I go into details of the principles, I want to show you a bit of the history of psychology. It appears to me that society missed out on a golden opportunity that could have provided a much healthier mental state for all to enjoy when they turned their backs on William James.

In the late 1800s to early 1900s, a man by the name of William James pointed to what looked like a truth. This truth goes something like this: with our mind, consciousness, and thought, we make up our entire reality and then we live in that reality. If we learn about these principles, we can live a much more fulfilling life where our inner reality will become one of no judgment of self or others, just curiosity and love of all that we are connected to. Psychology was really starting to put belief behind this information and it looked like this was the new direction for self-development.

Psychology was being looked at as an internal experience, that of thought, which caused an emotional reaction usually resulting in a behaviour. The inside-out experience of life, via thought, was causing people to either live happily or miserably.

If you could learn to have a quiet internal mind and feel grateful for what you have, then your thoughts will be more loving and peaceful. If you could learn to replace the inner negative thoughts with thoughts that make you feel better about yourself and others, then this will lead you to a healthier mental state. James showed people that they were whole and healthy inside and that they didn't need any fixing; they were not broken. People just needed to pay attention to the thoughts that served them well and stop believing or paying any attention to the thoughts that made them feel unwell inside.

James put forth the idea that the principles of mind, consciousness, and thought, when understood and used to our benefit, were all that we needed to be psychologically healthy. This could turn your life into one of feeling love and compassion for all others. Society at that time understood that we have consciousness and thought, but they asked James to prove that the mind existed. William James was distraught, as he could not yet prove that the mind existed. He moved away from the psychological community and stopped trying to tell society about these principles.

It was shortly after the principles of mind, consciousness, and thought had failed to produce scientific proof of the mind that Dr. Sigmund Freud came along. His theories revolved around thoughts that humans had a self and an ego and many inner conflicting beliefs and behaviours. He theorized that people needed a lot of fixing. Freud seemed to view people as quite broken psychologically, and he developed many theories as to why humans were so psychologically sick.

From the Freudian days, psychology has moved forward to develop some four hundred theories and treatments to help people with mental illness. There are many theories and treatments that might help, but none of them hold any guarantee that help will be found if you try them. Many people have found relief from their mental suffering through these psychological treatments and therapies, but there is still too much suffering being experienced by many.

What I see as a thread weaving through all of psychology, from Freudian days up to and including now, is that there is something deeply wrong with people. Our behaviours need to be changed and treated to try to make ourselves mentally healthier. The idea is that our experience of life comes from an outside event which affects us internally. This essentially means that our behaviours need to be changed and we need to receive treatment to learn of new behavior.

I am not a doctor and I do not ever advise people to go against their doctor's orders. However, I am a person who has experienced depression. I have also been given a diagnosis of depression, and I have taken medication for this. I feel very strongly that I have found more help to alleviate my depression through the three principles than any theory or treatment offered from the mainstream psychology in society today.

There are so many diagnoses made by psychiatrists and psychologists, and these diagnoses, or labels, grow in numbers every year. I recently heard that there is a label or diagnosis for excessive cell phone use. Creating more diagnoses and techniques to treat them does not seem to be the answer. We still see way too many suicides occurring, general unhappiness, and quiet desperation that many people live with on a daily basis.

People are living their lives and looking, on the outside, as if they are fine while being stressed and fearful of the thoughts going on in their heads. It is really necessary to find ways to relieve people from this inner pain and suffering. I can say, from experience, that if you have mental health issues and you learn how your thinking works, you may then change how you experience life.

There are oh so many ways to be unhappy, but there is only one way to be happy. If you put away all of your thinking and become quiet inside you can then respond to life from your inner quiet place of wisdom, which we all have. When you let go of judgment and most beliefs and most opinions, then you are free to see and feel your inner wisdom.

If you begin to understand how your thinking works, you will then see that you have the freedom to pay attention to only the thoughts you want to think about. If we go back to a time when psychology was going in a different direction, we see how hopeful life looked through the three principles, explained by William James and later by Sydney Banks. These two men were going in the right direction to show humanity a way to live with love and compassion for all others.

If society had followed the path of these two men, there may be many people living more peaceful lives inside of themselves. It is very important to see that we experience life from the inside-out, not the outside-in.

The outside-in theory gives individual or group therapy where you go over painful situations. You talk about them, try to understand them, and try to understand your behaviour so you can change the behaviour. This, I believe, is the belief of most present-day psychology.

However, if you take on the view of the three principles, when you have a painful experience, you may need to tell someone what happened. But, once you have told what happened, you are then free to let go of the experience. It is in the past; it is gone. It sure isn't here in the present moment; it is just a memory. You can move on to a new thought or memory, or you can just be quiet inside with no need to worry or give attention to the unpleasant thoughts.

If you do have a memory of someone doing something terribly wrong to you, it is important that you forgive that person. I think it is a fact that people are not evil. Instead, they are usually afraid. This fear shows up as anger, and then misguided behaviours are the result. People act from what their thinking is causing them to believe is true, and then they believe they must act on that misguided thought.

When people do wrong or hurtful things to one another it is because they are misguided in their thinking. You may never be able to forgive the act that caused you pain or hurt. You don't have to forgive the act or the behaviour; just forgive the person by understanding they were and maybe still are misguided in their beliefs and their thoughts.

It is for your own peace of mind that you must forgive others, and then you can go on to heal. Once you realize that they didn't know any better way to act at that time, you are free to move away from the experience and you no longer feel like a victim. Forgiving them gives you back your freedom: you don't have to feel like a victim.

After an external event happens, I don't believe you need to go over that horrible event many times so that you can learn a new response to it. The principles, explained quite eloquently by Sydney Banks, would say you don't have to relive the experience over and over; this is neither necessary nor helpful. Once the experience is over, it then becomes a memory.

You never have to relive a memory over and over unless it is a pleasant one and you want to. If it is an unpleasant memory, you let it go. It honestly doesn't matter what happened in the past; you are absolutely able to let it rest as a part of the past. I can assure you that we all have an inner energy, our mind, that is never damaged no matter what has happened. This I know from an experience of sexual assault in my early teenage years. That experience is certainly not here in the moment; it is gone and now just a memory. I could let it affect me and my life, but I choose to see it as gone, in the past, just a memory. This leaves me free to no longer have any fear and anger over this event and I no longer need to have feelings of inferiority and self-loathing. I was able recently to forgive the individuals but, I will probably never forgive their behavior. Just forgiving the males involved gave me a new freedom. The forgiveness is for me to move on and be free of the experience, it is not for them at all.

It is from this inner wisdom, or energy, that you forgive others. There is no fear, no judgment, and no lack of confidence at this inner level of wisdom that we all have. The three principles of mind, consciousness, and thought will awaken you to a new way of experiencing your life.

Experiencing mind, consciousness, and thought at a deep level is achieved by getting quiet inside of yourself and listening for your inner wisdom. It is never about looking outside of yourself to find the path to resolving your inner conflicts. This inner wisdom can also be thought of as that intuition that sometimes surfaces. If you can recall times that you just intuitively knew what you should do in a difficult situation, well, that is your inner wisdom, or your mind, speaking to you.

Your inner wisdom will always guide you, if you listen and let it in. If you get quiet inside of your head, then your inner thoughts can come from your inner wisdom. When we are feeling judgmental, or self-conscious, or just plain uncomfortable inside, then usually it is just that noise in our head talking loudly. I call this noise your intellectual thinking which results from your opinions and beliefs. True wisdom holds pretty much no opinions or judgments. A lot of inner chatter is usually just going to mess you up with ideas that are not coming from your true inner wisdom or your mind.

Most of our creative and helpful thoughts come from our true wisdom, or universal mind, or universal intelligence. In contrast, many people will go their whole lives mostly just thinking from their intellect or their personal mind where they only have access to information that is learned in this life and now held in the brain as a memory. To get to your really interesting thoughts, your truly creative mind, you must access the universal mind. You do this by learning to quiet your mind.

You are now on your way to realizing that your unhealthy thoughts don't have to mean anything at all; they are not usually true or helpful for you to reach the best solution. Most people do not realize that most of their thoughts do not require an action. They think that if they have a thought, they have to act on that thought. Yet you do not need to react to most of your thoughts. This leads to the realization that often we can turn away from our thoughts; often nothing needs to be done. We don't have to believe most of our thoughts.

We have between sixty thousand to one hundred thousand thoughts per day and we just let most of them slide on through us; we don't give them our attention. It is when we stop on an unpleasant thought that we get ourselves into trouble. Maybe the thought that you stop on is, "I am a useless person," and then you start to feel like a useless person. You may start acting like a useless person. You mistakenly believe the thought because you thought it, so it must be true. Now you are acting like a useless person.

The truth is that thoughts are not necessarily true; you may just need to ignore the thoughts that don't serve you well. Once you learn to let the unwanted thought pass through your head, you can then begin stopping on the thoughts that serve you well and just simply ignore the thoughts that are not good for you.

So, to recap this chapter, we discussed the beginning of formal psychology. Based on the belief of William James in the 1890-1910, we operate in life with mind, consciousness, and thought. We create our reality in life, one thought at a time. Society liked this view and was starting to get behind Mr. James on these principles, seeing them as being of utmost importance in a psychologically healthy life.

Then Sigmund Freud, a psychiatrist in the early 1900s, proposed a new psychological idea that we all behave the way we do because we have unresolved conflicts stemming from unhealthy attachment to our mother or father. Freud developed therapy with free association of words and lots of talking about our inadequate selves and our egos. He felt that most people were sick and broken. These psychologically sick people needed to talk through any and all of these mixed-up thoughts and learn new behaviours. From there, psychology developed into the four hundred therapies and treatments we see today. The outside-in (mainstream psychology) experience of life works to make some people feel somewhat better inside some of the time.

Today we are beginning to grasp the idea that there is a lot more to humans and the psychological experience in life than these theories would suggest. Through understanding that we have an inner thought which creates an emotion and an outer reaction, we can begin to really change our inner world of thoughts. This is how we change our life by changing our thoughts. Michael Neill has written a great book entitled The Inside-Out Revolution. This book explains our life as we experience our inner thoughts and create our outer world with this inside-out understanding.

We live with an inner knowledge or mind at a certain level of consciousness or awareness, and we have thoughts that create emotions and resulting behaviour. Through these principles we can either live in love and happiness, or we can end up living in fear and sadness. It is through understanding our mind that we begin to see a spiritual side to ourselves, as you will see in the next chapter.

In the past, I believe people were fearful of looking at themselves as spiritual beings. This may be because of their belief that spiritual meant an unknown, maybe even spooky, something that they could not see. It is just the opposite of that.

Learning that our spiritual side is full of divine gifts makes me feel very humble. Our spiritual side is just energy, more specifically universal energy. Everything is made of and from energy. Physics has shown this to be true, without a doubt. There was a time when there was just energy; no planets existed. The universe was just energy. The universe is energy, and energy was able to, over time, learn to evolve and combine to create mass.

The physics theory of the Big Bang suggests that energy figured out how to combine or attach and create mass. It was from this event that planets eventually evolved into being and organisms evolved and became more complex. But, unquestionably, we are all made of this energy and mass because everything is made from this universal energy. We are here in spirit (or energy) and body (or energy in the form of mass), and so we are of the formless (energy) and the form (mass or body). The reality of body (form) and energy (formless) or spirit is also at the foundation of the three principles.

In the next chapter we look at the three principles of mind, consciousness, and thought. We see how these three divine gifts, created through universal energy, are available for all humans to live with and love themselves and their life through. It is very exciting to understand and internalize the idea that we are energy in the form (body or mass) and formless (spirit or energy) just the same as the universe is energy. We all have a little of the universal energy in and through us at all times. There is evidence that this energy that we are made of has an intelligence to it.

CHAPTER 3

The Three Principles of Mind, Consciousness, and Thought

"All creatures, great or small,
interpret what they think of life
via these three divine gifts."

Quotation from *The Missing
Link* by Sydney Banks

To understand the principles, you first need to listen to and observe a good feeling inside as I try to tell you about them. To try to feel this inner peace, I want you to think of a happy time in your life. You can go back to your childhood, or later in life, and recall a time when you felt safe and happy. Close your eyes and think of a peaceful, happy memory. Imagine it in detail; recall what the day was like. Were you outside? Did you feel the warmth of the sun? What was happening around you and inside of you?

See if you can feel that memory in your belly. Recall it, sit with it, and just feel it inside. This inner state of well-being is yours; it is your birthright to feel good inside. You can live with this good feeling of love, of safety, and of happiness. You can be reassured to know that all that you seek is right inside of you and has been there all the time.

That peaceful, contented feeling inside of you is the principles and they way they can touch your inner soul. You will seek this feeling as you begin to understand the principles. Understanding the principles will give you hope for attaining whatever you might need as you move into your future, one day at a time.

You will raise your level of consciousness or your ability to perceive the world. With a high level of consciousness and a high level of thought or thoughts that serve you well, you then become able to access unbelievable wisdom from your mind. You will access wisdom that you probably never knew you had. This wisdom is your universal mind.

You see, once you understand that you are truly wise with access to all of the wisdom in the universe, you will begin to see that you are whole and healthy inside. You can handle and accomplish anything you want to. Your inner energy is a healthy state inside of you that has always been there. Understanding that you have a personal mind, or intelligence from education and parents, and a universal mind, or intelligence of all that has been learned since the beginning of time, will start to give you an idea of what a divine individual you really are.

No matter where you have come from or where you are going in your life, when you change your thoughts you will change your life. All of your life is developed one thought at a time. Realizing this will show you that as you think, your thoughts become your reality. So if you think, "I can never get ahead in life; I am always broke," then this is what your mind hears and will bring about in your life. But if you think, "I am grateful for all that I have and I know opportunities to become loving and financially stable will present themselves to me," then your mind hears this and you should expect opportunities to present themselves to you.

Once you are consciously looking for the opportunities that you know are going to come your way, then they will start showing up in your life. Your thoughts and your consciousness will be at a higher level. The other wonderful thing is that you won't miss the good things coming your way because you will be expecting them. I missed a lottery win once because I just wasn't expecting it, become willing to expect the good things!

As good things start to happen to you, you will feel more positive about your life. This positivity will increase your confidence and your hope and you will feel better inside. It is true that as soon as you stop looking on the outside and blaming others for a lack of success, you will start to feel your inner peace. Sit quietly with a peaceful mind and you will get that wonderful feeling inside. This feeling will lead you to experience peace and contentment; some call it love for self and others.

You can ask any questions and be silent, and then the answer or insight will eventually come into your mind in the form of thought. You see, with mind, consciousness, and thought there is personal thought and universal thought and so it is with each one of these principles. Once you accept and have faith in the principles, you will change; you will walk and talk with more confidence and people will notice that you have changed.

As you learn more about the principles, you will see that they are the answer to all of psychology, philosophy, theology, and physics. They give you the answers to all of the questions you might have asked and want to ask about life. With this understanding, you will see that you are whole; you were never broken. You can live life with joy, love, and understanding for all others.

It matters what you have been through in life, but your past can be left behind you. You can learn to live in your present moment and not worry about the future. The past is gone, the future hasn't arrived yet, and we only have the present moment to live in. The present is where you will strive to live from moment to moment in your life.

As you move into a healthier life, there are some things from the past to leave behind. If you have happy memories, then enjoy them sometimes, in your thoughts. If you have unpleasant memories from the past, do not dwell on them. What can we learn from the principles about letting go of the past?

When bad things happen to us, it is our normal response to feel like a victim. In these circumstances when someone has done something harmful to you or said something hurtful, the tendency is to be angry at that person and resent them and feel victimized. But the only person who is really being hurt by this is the person feeling victimized. This anger takes up a lot of good mental energy and makes you bitter inside. You cannot move to being happier when you are bitter and angry.

The anger will disappear when you find forgiveness in you. You need to forgive the person who has wronged you. That does not mean that you ever have to forgive the behaviour, but it is so important, for your health, to forgive that person who wronged you. This forgiveness will rid you of the anger and resentment and let you move on to a more peaceful mind. You must also understand that the person was doing the best they knew how to do at that time in their life. We are all at different points of development in our lives. The first necessary step to living more peacefully is to learn to quiet the mind, but I think everyone goes through this path with whatever step they choose next for themselves. My journey will be very different from any other person's journey.

To develop yourself into living in a healthier state of mind, the three principles will show you that it is important to begin to understand your inner mind, your consciousness, and your thoughts. They are your inner energy or your inner spirit, whichever you choose to call them. Your inner divine gifts are your mind, your consciousness, and your thoughts.

To give you a bit of a better understanding of what they are, the mind is your intelligence. We all have a personal intelligence or personal mind, a universal intelligence or universal mind, and personal thought and universal thought. Of course, our universal consciousness is of personal and universal knowledge.

Your personal intelligence is all that you learn from your family, school, and society or all that the brain stores from learned knowledge since your birth. Your universal intelligence or universal mind, however, is all of the knowledge the universe holds of past, present, and future. Imagine that you, a divine human, have access to the knowledge of the universe. You are probably asking, "How can that be?" In the following chapter on the mind, I go into further detail about this. For now, suffice it to say that the mind is a wonderful energy and intelligence to have access to.

You also have access to your consciousness, which is your awareness of your surrounding environment. We have many levels of consciousness and I believe we only understand some of these levels as humans here on Earth. Our consciousness can be at the level of low or high, depending on our thought at any given time. Our consciousness can also be personal or universal. For example, if you were on your way to a beach, you might be aware that it is a gorgeous, sunny day to go for a swim. If you felt happy and were looking forward to the day, you would be at a high level of consciousness: happy and content. Our level of consciousness is important and affects how we feel. Does it affect our thoughts?

Yes, our thoughts are affected by our level of consciousness. If your thought is, "I hate life," then your level of consciousness will be low. This is a rather negative thought which leads to a low level of consciousness and possibly a poor view of your life.

We do know that our thoughts are definitely a big part of becoming a psychologically healthy person. Understanding the principles will show you a way to live with unconditional love and gratitude for your life. This understanding will show you that there is no need to judge others, as no one really knows what another person's existence is like.

Judgment usually leads to gossip, and neither of these ways of being are useful in a meaningful life. Let others live and know that they are doing the best they know how to do at that time. Letting go of feeling like a victim in your life and letting go of anger and judgment will free up a lot of energy to put to better use.

So, to recap the principles: mind is our intelligence, consciousness is our awareness, and thoughts are the ideas that flow through our head. We can now see what makes up the three principles. There are no necessary treatments and there are no necessary techniques that you are required to go through to live life through the three principles.

You just need to be prepared to raise your level of thoughts, raise your level of consciousness, and become peaceful so you can listen to your mind. Then, your life will improve immensely. You will be well on your way to a better life where you can be free of the ideas that held you in mental distress.

Understanding your thoughts gives you free will. You will be free to choose the thoughts that will get your attention. This will free you to create the life that you choose to have. Your mind, consciousness, and thought all come from the energy of the universe. Just like gravity is a principle so are mind, consciousness, and thought.

In calling these three concepts principles, you must understand that this means they are truths, not theories. We cannot see gravity, or feel it, or smell it, or taste it, or touch it, yet we accept that gravity is a scientific fact, a force that exists. So too are our mind, consciousness, and thought.

Our mind, consciousness, and thought are scientific principles. We understand this through physics, philosophy, and any other science you may wish to apply them to. They are divine principles that can lift you away from mental anguish and show you just how perfect you already are, right now.

It doesn't matter where you are in life; everything is okay. There is nowhere else that you should be; there is nothing different that you should have done. The present moment is the perfect place for you to be in. Everything happens for a reason, although you may not always see the big picture. You have to let life unfold for this.

You posses a divine inner knowledge and wisdom that can take you through anything that comes up in life. No one is wiser than you and no one is wiser than me; we all have the same access to the wisdom of the universe. The inner wisdom you have can lead you back to the perfectly healthy inner state of psychological well-being that has always been there. This will allow you to live with joy, gratitude, and love for self and others. Will you take this knowledge and apply it to your inner self?

You have to see and internalize that we are made up of energy. Your reality is created because you have the energy of the principles of mind, consciousness, and thought. It is true that science has proven that all energy and matter have come from the universal energy. Science, or specifically physics, has shown us that everything in the universe has come from energy. To see this, I want you to think back to when the universe was only energy. There were no planets, no sun, and no stars. There was only energy, and that energy was the universe.

Then, as physics shows us, energy combined to make mass. Many questions arise from this occurrence. How did energy form to create mass? Well, energy has wisdom, or intelligence. This energy, which then developed mass, went on to create planets and stars. Involution, or ideas, and evolution followed that bring us to today, with such complex developments as humans and many solar systems within the universe. Wow, it is a divine multitude of evolved and evolving occurrences.

And, here we are, each one of us, living in this wonderful energy and mass. It is interesting to note that all energy also vibrates at a certain frequency. A person feeling unconditional love vibrates at the highest frequency level and a person feeling hate vibrates at the lowest frequency. Our emotions cause our inner energy to vibrate at different frequencies.

The thoughts flowing through our head can cause emotions. In turn, these emotions cause vibrations of energy with higher or lower frequency, depending on the emotion being experienced. We are made up of formless energy, or spirit and energy in form, body, or mass. We are made up of both form and formless energy. Yes, we all have a bit of the universe inside of us, and what a meaningful experience we can have here on Earth if we truly understand this.

If everything evolved from energy and mass, then we have an inner energy or spirit or formless part of us and we also have a mass to us, comprised of our body. So we live in a form or a body, which is mass that comes from energy. We have a formless inner energy, because everything comes from energy. Thus, we are part energy and part mass. We are of the form and the formless. We are made up of the same things as the universe, or, to put it another way, we have a little of the universe inside of us.

We call this inner energy our divine spirit, or our soul, or our inner wisdom. We all have it. How do we know that everything has mind, consciousness, and thought? Books have been written about this. For right now, all we need to understand is that the universal energy flows in and through us as it flows in and through everything. We are made of mass, which is just energy combined to create mass. This is our body. We are partly comprised of pure energy or spirit.

Some choose to call this energy divine, universal energy; some call it God; and some call it the divine spirit. It doesn't matter what you call it, as it is all really the same thing. It acknowledges that there is a divine powerful energy with an intelligence to it. It is true that universal energy is neutral. It has no stake in good or bad; it is energy.

The universe is neither good nor bad; it has only the capability to be and to vibrate at different levels with the help of consciousness and thought. Feelings of love cause a vibration within us that vibrates at the highest frequency level. Hate vibrates at the lowest frequency level.

If you have negative thoughts, you will have vibrations at low level frequencies. If you have positive thoughts, you will have energy vibrations and frequencies at high levels inside of you. If you feel happy, then your energy will vibrate at a higher frequency, and if you feel love, then your energy will vibrate at the highest possible frequency. Our emotions create energy vibrations at very different levels.

There is energy vibrating at different frequencies in you. The higher vibrations are the good feelings, while the lower vibrations are that of hate or anger. These are the negative thoughts. There is no duality to life, there is no good versus evil, there is no heaven versus hell, and there is definitely no devil, as some believe. Everything came from energy. We are energy or the formless or spirit of ourselves, and mass, which is energy, combines to create mass: our body. The energy is divine, as it has great wisdom, it is conscious, and it has thought. This energy that flows in and between us also connects us to one another.

The energy of the universe is neutral, not good or evil. People can act in horrible ways and it doesn't make them evil. Horrific behaviour is simply misguided people acting on misguided thoughts. There is no evil, no devil, and no hell (unless you create your own hell on Earth with misguided thoughts and behaviours). So, we have a massive universe made of energy, and then energy, or universal mind, figured out how to combine and create mass. It was able to do this because it has a wisdom or intelligence to it. Physics, now aware of this consciousness and wisdom, agrees there is a knowing to the energy of the universe, which is also the energy that flows in us.

With mind, consciousness, and thought occurring in the form (mass or body) and the formless (energy or spirit) state, we can all feel pretty fabulous about living as universal energy and mass. We all have the ability to be capable of some pretty awesome things in this life. Think about it for a minute: we are one with the universe. Just as a drop of water can be separated from the ocean, a drop of spirit can be separated from the universe to become you or me.

We are truly divine in our presence with energy or spirit. Seeing that we have mind, both personal and universal; consciousness, also both personal and universal; and thought, both personal and universal, these concepts guide us through our life every day. If you feel grateful, let go of victim-mode and refuse to judge others. Then, you will start to feel really confident and healthy inside. Using your thoughts to better your life and live in the present moment means that you are well on your way to living the three principles.

CHAPTER 4

Mind

> "Every human mind has direct access to its experience here on Earth, and the human mind always has access to its own spiritual roots…. from whence it came."
>
> Quotation from *The Missing Link* by Sydney Banks

The mind is, as Sydney Banks refers to it, both personal and universal. The personal mind is that information stored by the brain. The universal mind is the knowledge or wisdom that the universe has evolved to or through. This knowledge is always updating and changing or being added to with evolution and involution. This means that every human being who is alive at the time has the same access to all of the wisdom the universe holds. Some people may go through their lives and not know they are in fact very wise. They may occasionally and accidently access their universal wisdom and carry on none the wiser to their universal wisdom.

What a lot more fun it is to know when and how you are accessing this wisdom and knowledge. There are times when it would be so helpful to have access to this mind that you possess. For example, when you are having trouble making a decision, what if you could go to your universal mind to get answers?

You can do this if you can get out of your own way and quit spinning your wheels and trying so hard to get answers. The answers to any question you may have are available to you, if you can just learn to get quiet inside. It sounds so easy to just get quiet inside.

Our inner self is often so busy with thoughts coming and going all of the time that it can be a bit more difficult to access the quiet mind. However, I did not say it is impossible. It takes practice to quiet your mind. Learn to sit quietly with nothing on your mind; do this every chance you get. This will lead to a peaceful mind. It will also lead to accessing your universal mind and your personal mind. Both minds are the same in universal mind, so you have access to both when you get quiet inside of your head. Some people like to meditate to learn the art of getting quiet inside.

When I first heard this, I thought, "I don't want to meditate and I don't know how to meditate. Do I really have to do this?" I have since found out that meditation is not as difficult or time-consuming as I had thought. When I learned to quiet my mind, I practiced the following simple meditation: sit or lay down and count from one to one hundred. Breathe in through your nose, fairly deeply, then hold for a few seconds and breathe out through your mouth slowly. That is number one. Wait, and when you are ready, breathe in and out again with nothing on your mind. It may feel boring, but at about fifty you should begin to feel somewhat relaxed. Carry on to one hundred with no thoughts on your mind. The counting helps to stop the thinking.

Now that you are learning to get quiet inside, you will begin see what a wonderful way this is to live. The truth is that there is really nothing you need to do except quiet your head of chatter; you do not have to meditate to achieve this. You may have accessed your universal mind without even realizing it. In my experience, I accessed the universal mind many times when I was a young child between the ages of four and six. Then life got a hold of me and I began to believe the things I heard others say about who I was. As a youngster, I was spiritually in tune with my universal mind. It would just flow in me and through me, creating a beautiful, peaceful feeling of love for life and others.

I recall being at my grandma's farm. While walking down the path to her garden, I just started chattering about what a beautiful day it was and how I loved the shadows stretching across the path. The sun was shining so bright and warming me, and I said that I just felt so at home when I was there. My sister asked, "What are you talking about? You are usually so quiet." And back to reality I came, where I remembered that I was shy and quiet.

I quietly wondered, "Where did all of that joy and chatter come from?" I recall that moment like it was yesterday. Universal mind can shine through at any time if you are quiet and open to it.

In another experience, I accessed my universal mind when I was eight years old. I had no clue what had happened to allow me to access this knowledge that I was able to access. At the time I lived in a small town and there was always a feeling of being safe no matter where I went in that town. Nothing out of the ordinary happened there, at least not that I knew about.

The day I will tell you about was a beautiful sunny day and all was well with me and in my world. I had just crossed through the hospital parking lot and passed through the back lane to reach the street. I was walking down the sidewalk when I heard gravel spinning from tires on a car. I turned around to see what was going on and out flew a dark brown car from the back lane, onto the street. The brakes screeched to a stop beside me and a tall, thin man sat with his eyes fixed on me. I could tell he was very tall because he had to bend his head sideways to look at me out of his open window. He casually said, "It's a hot day; jump in and I'll drive you home." I just stared back at him and no words would come out of my mouth. Then he said, "Come on, hop in; I'll take you for ice cream before I take you home."

I was so startled by what was happening, and finally I said, "No, I am going right here." And, with that statement, I then turned away and walked toward the house that happened to be right beside me.

As I walked up the sidewalk, I thought, "What if there is no one home? Who lives here, anyway?" I took two steps up toward the veranda and changed my mind, turned, and raced behind the house. From there I ran toward the hedge and crouched down, trying to get as small as I could.

He was still there in his car, on the other side of the hedge. I thought, "I have no idea what to do, so I will just be very quiet, breathe quietly, and sit still." What seemed like an eternity passed and finally I could hear his tires start to turn on the gravel and he was slowly rolling away in his car.

The next thing I could see was his car turning and going onto the next street. I again asked myself, "What do I do now?" And the suggestion appeared just like words arising in my head: RUN. So I darted out from the yard and started running as fast as I could. I stopped to check for cars and I could see his car down the street. I thought he might have seen me, so as quick as I could I crossed the street and ran for home. I reached a hill and thought, "I can't go any farther." I was panting from running. The thought came, "You can and will run; keep going." I was running and getting slower and thinking, "I cannot go any farther; I can't keep going." Then the thought came, "Run, run like a rabbit." I said to myself, "Whaaaaaaat...? How?" These answers just came to me as a thought running through my head would normally come. However, I knew it was a knowing beyond what I had acquired knowledge of in my brain.

Then I started running, springing off my toes and sprinting, cupping my hands in an unfamiliar way. The wind was suddenly rushing faster and faster by my cheeks; faster and faster I ran. There was no fear; I was simply doing what needed to be done. Running like a rabbit and I had no idea how to do that, it just unfolded and movements that I could not explain happened. Imagine that: I had never run fast before yet I was moving like a bullet and no fear inside of me while this horrible experience was unfolding! There was just focus and a totally quiet mind.

I saw the brown car on the next street over and I knew it was him. I had the thought, "Faster, go faster," and that's just what I was somehow able to do. I reached my home and yard and had the thought, "Hit the ground right here; lay down here." So I hit the ground and asked in my head, "Why here? Why lay down here?" I had these words flow through me, "Here, because there is a small dip down in the ground and he won't be able to see you here." I was not using knowledge that I had in my brain, there was a higher knowing or knowledge that was guiding me, this was something that I had no understanding of, at that time. It was very clear to me that I was being protected and guided by something, I just had no explanation of what that was, at that time. I heard the car stop in front of my house as I lay there panting for breath. I lay there, trying again to be still and quiet. After a few minutes, his car started to roll forward slowly, and then he sped away. I was safe now; it was over.

He hadn't been able to get near me or abduct me, but he had stalked me and chased me. It was at this moment that my thoughts started running, "What if he had gotten me? What would he have done to me? Where did those answers about what to do come from?" With these thoughts I began to feel very frightened. Feelings of fear overcame me and I started to shake and shudder at the thought of what might have happened. What had just happened?

I spent many years not really knowing where that knowledge came from of what I should do in that situation. I did not know why all fear fell away as I moved through the actions of overcoming the problem at hand. It wasn't until many years later, as I understood the three principles, that I came to fully understand what happened that day.

Quite simply, I had become very quiet and asked the question, "What should I do?" As I sat quietly, the answers unfolded for me from the universal mind. Though I did not realize what I was doing, I called on universal mind and stayed quiet and the answers came. Answers to any questions you have are available anytime you need them if you get very quiet inside of your head. This wisdom and these answers are available to everyone, any time you need them. That is the remarkable thing about our mind and this knowing and understanding we have available to us. You are never alone; the universal energy or universal mind is always there to help you if you need help.

This is huge because it also means that you do not have to live in fear of the unknown. Imagine living with no fear; wouldn't that be great? It is true that there is really nothing to the fear that we all experience at times. Your universal mind can assist you to move above and beyond and lose those feelings of fear completely. I was very fortunate to have the help I needed right there and then on that day.

I know that I can access my mind, consciousness, and thought. Be it personal or universal, it is there to help navigate life's difficulties if I just get quiet inside and ask. This is such a comfort for me. Yet even with this knowledge I can still get caught up in the moment and have some fear run my life until I get quiet and stop the thought storm in my head. The universal mind is where all of the creative thinking comes from.

If you recall, I explained how the inside-out experience of life works. You have a thought followed by an emotional response, and then usually a behaviour follows that. Well, you have the ability to stop at the thought and just let it go. You don't have to proceed from the thought on to the emotion. We really just make up that emotion anyway, as I was able to show you in my near abduction experience. All fear fell away as I just lived in the moment and moved through what had to be done.

In fact, this is how we make up our lives. With a thought, an emotion, and a behaviour, we create our lives. That means that by changing or not paying attention to the thought, we can change the direction of our lives. It is necessary to recognize that it takes the combination of mind, consciousness, and thought to complete the circuit of life experience. The mind, or intelligence, has the wisdom to answer all of the questions we might have in life. We are just as capable as anyone of accessing this divine gift.

Learn to get quiet inside, to access your divine gift of the universal mind. You must also know that no one is wiser than you. You have access to all of the knowledge of the universe. Connect with it and learn to live insightfully. The mind is the place of all creative thought generation.

Your mind is capable of giving you the answers to solve whatever difficulties arise in your life. If you stop the chatter of the personal mind and listen for the universal mind, you will be capable of moving through any decision that you have to make.

CHAPTER 5

Consciousness

"As our consciousness [or awareness] descends we lose our feelings of love and understanding and experience a world of emptiness, bewilderment and despair."

Quotation from *The Missing Link* by Sydney Banks

Consciousness is our ability to perceive the world around us. Without our consciousness, we cannot be involved in our life. There are many levels of consciousness we can show up with in our life, for example if a person felt angry and proceeded to harm another human being by punching them in the face simply because they didn't like the look on that stranger's face. This would be at a low level of consciousness, with the person throwing the punch feeling angry and probably having some angry thoughts which he acted on by harming another human being.

If you have thoughts of harming yourself or others, then these are not loving thoughts. These are considered thoughts that are at a low level of consciousness. When you have thoughts of love and gratitude, then these thoughts are at a high level of consciousness. There are many levels of consciousness between these two examples.

The more you can live with thoughts that are at a high level of consciousness, the better your actions and decisions will be. Another way of explaining this concept of consciousness would be to say that at the lowest level of consciousness, thoughts are of murder or suicide, and at the highest level of consciousness, thoughts are of unconditional love for all and gratitude for all that we have in life. Does reading these words give you a nice feeling inside?

If it is a nice feeling that you feel in your stomach, these are the three principles in action. That's really what it's all about. When you learn a little about these principles and you feel nice inside, you can be assured that you are getting an understanding of your mind, consciousness, and thought.

In attempting to share this knowledge of the principles, it is often said that words don't really help to convey the true meaning. It is true that words are not often enough to truly explain these ways of being in your life. The universe has gifted me with some life experiences of how this works, and I will share a bit more of what I have experienced.

I have had a couple of head injuries in the past. The first injury was at about the age of ten. When I was running, I slipped, fell, hit my head on a step, and knocked myself out. I was unconscious and then suddenly I was at the hospital. I was aware of my surroundings but not able to respond to anything. I was in a coma. I could clearly hear what was being said by the doctor and my mom; I just couldn't respond.

If someone is in a coma, they may hear everything that is said around them. I could hear the doctor say, "She's in a coma right now and we need to get her back into consciousness." Then I heard my mom sniffling and thought, "Oh, she's crying." Interestingly, this didn't scare me or upset me, though normally that would have upset me to hear her cry. I just felt love inside of me. This altered state of consciousness left me unable to experience normal emotions of sadness, it seemed to me. The doctor placed smelling salts under my nose. Let me tell you that's a bad smell, but this brought me right out of that coma immediately.

I can still recall the burn that accompanied that smell. So, we know that my sense of smell worked. I had my senses of smell, touch, and hearing intact, but not the normal emotional reaction. I find that interesting. In a normal state of consciousness you have your senses and emotional reactions intact, but in a coma your senses are intact but emotions don't seem to exist as they normally would. I also felt no pain from the physical injury. It was like experiencing my spiritual self only. The present state of my body and physical pain were just not present. It was a calm, peaceful sense of being present with feelings of love and absolutely no worries of any kind.

I felt no sadness when my mom cried, yet I felt love for her. I experienced no fear or confusion in the coma state. While out of the coma I was confused and fearful, like the experience of personal consciousness or the form of human feelings. The coma state seemed to be the universal consciousness or feeling of spirit only. In this state there was no human or body experience of fear and pain; instead, only love was present.

My theory is that we are placed on this Earth as form (body) and formless (spirit) beings to experience all of the possible range of emotions there are to experience. I believe that is the purpose of our life, as we know it, here on Earth. Emotions might be the ingredient that is added to the mix when a human is formed in the body and spirit combination, the form and formless state.

I believe we are here to experience all of the possible emotions available to us because in the experience of head injury number one, this altered state of consciousness was void of emotions except love. Now, in the experience of head injury number two, I had a totally different altered state of consciousness. With this head injury I had a near-death experience. I fell, smacked my head on ice, and knocked myself out AGAIN. This injury was at forty-six years of age.

This time I was unconscious and then some kind of awareness came to be. I was in a dark place and thought, "It's very dark; where am I?" It was like seeing without the eyes. Then there was a feeling of knowing this place. I felt no fear. I was just there. There was no containment of my body in this state; my spirit was without my body. I had this very clear feeling and understanding of expansion of energy in all directions. It felt like I went on forever. My spirit just flowed, endlessly expanding with no beginning and no end. There was a content and peaceful feeling, just like that of love, flowing in the energy that was me.

I was in a flow, or a wave of being, that just carried me. It was so peaceful and I was so content; I had no worries whatsoever, just a feeling of love. I was so relaxed and comfortable and thought that I could just stay there forever. I felt like I was in the perfect place and could just bask in this comforting feeling. I was so, so content just being right there. I had no need for anything; I had absolutely everything I could want or need right here in this existence. I existed in energy, there was no mass of any kind to be contained in, and nothing was wanted or needed.

Just being me in formless energy was purely a divine place to flow in and live out eternity in. I felt completely happy to accept this as home. I was completely settled and needed nothing more in this present flow and feeling.

Then there was a bright light coming toward me. It seemed fine with me that this light was getting closer and closer. I thought, "Oh, my girls need me." And with that thought, my eyes shot open and I was back in form, in body and formless spirit. I was immediately startled at the reality that I couldn't breathe; I was starving for oxygen. My legs were lying across my chest and over my shoulder, and I couldn't get a breath.

I was able to scream the thought in my head to get my legs down off of my chest. After what seemed like an eternity, finally my legs lifted and fell down to the ground with a thud. I got myself breathing, and then I just lay there breathing rhythmically and deeply in and out.

After that fall, I had a lot of trouble with headaches and dizziness and memory loss for a long while; to this day I still have some memory difficulties. It altered my life very dramatically for years to come. This horrific injury made me feel like a victim and I found myself asking questions like, "Why did this have to happen to me?"

Feeling like life was unfairly giving me impossible obstacles to overcome, I could no longer work in my career as a nurse. There were many days when parenting was so difficult. Taking care of things like cleaning at home was a challenge for me, and following steps to make a meal was very tough. I was definitely in victim mode.

Then, many years later, I found the three principles to guide me back to a healthy life. I found the three principles online in an ad for a course offered by Nicola Bird. For an entire week, I must have read everything of Sydney Banks that I could get my hands on. I learned and understood so many things in my life in a completely different way.

I realized that blessings had come from this injury. I had so much more time with my daughters and my husband. I had no choice but to slow down, and the stress from my nursing career was removed from my life. I went through very difficult times during my recovery from that head injury, but there were also some wonderful things that came along as a result of my head injury.

The time I spent in that state of unconsciousness showed me a whole different state to exist in: the state of energy or spirit. It was something so special it is hard to articulate, but it was the most desirable state I have ever been in. I am not afraid to go back there if that is death.

What stuck with me from the experience I had while unconscious were the wonderful feelings of peace and love; nothing else mattered. I think I experienced myself in formlessness, just energy, my spirit.

If there is a place you want to be and experience someday, it is in your pure energy or spirit. To be a part of the energy of the universe, in the pure energy state, to be without the experience of my body, to be present in just the formless energy, mind, or spirit, was astonishingly beautiful. It was a place that I am not ever afraid to return to. Because of this experience, I no longer fear death as being the end of me. I know that it will always be okay when I lose my form, as my formlessness or energy will continue on in the universe. No matter what happens, it will always be okay.

I can assure you that you will be okay too, no matter what happens. You and I will someday leave our form and go back to being in the formless energy. We will only be spirit. We will never cease to exist in the energy or formless state. We will leave our body behind, but our energy or our spirit will live on forever in the universe. Our consciousness, mind, and thought in the form and formless are divine. These gifts in only spirit are remarkable to experience, and, when combined with our mass or our body, our time here on Earth should be loving, happy, and blissful.

Living here on Earth where the form and formless combine to make up a human being is an experience that we can either take great delight in or we can live in misery. My experience has shown me that when we are in purely spiritual formlessness, we can experience feeling love but no other emotions. As I mentioned earlier, I have had these experiences and they have led me to the understanding that our existence as a human is ultimately to be here to experience all of the range of emotions possible while we are here.

I have concluded that we are placed here as humans to experience and react to all of the range of emotions available to us. We are capable of feeling happy, sad, angry, lonely, fearful, or whatever emotion we can imagine. This is just a thought in our conscious state. Maybe we are placed here in the form and formless to learn how to experience and react to all of these emotions. We don't know what is next. I do know we leave the body and our spirit returns to the universe. Maybe our spirit returns here in another form, or maybe we go somewhere else; I don't know.

The cosmic joke to this would be that we make up all of those feelings, with the exception of love which is a pure state bigger than an emotion, with our principle of personal thought. We worry, cause ourselves stress, and feel so much fear. Honestly, there is no fear or any of those other emotions. We make them all up, with the exception of love. Our personal consciousness has our emotions mixed in with it; our universal consciousness, minus our form, does not have our emotions mixed in with it. Our universal consciousness has only love available to experience when we are in the state of pure spirit, without body state.

If we have a thought and then an emotion, does that make the thought or the emotion real? No, the emotion we feel is just made up to fit with the thought we made up. If we make both of these up in our head, then why do we take them so seriously? A made-up thought can be true, but it is not necessarily true.

If we believe that we have no confidence and we feel bad inside when we are around other people, then we start to believe the thought that we have no confidence. But the thought of no confidence was a made-up thought because we can just as easily be told by ourselves or others that we are confident, and then that becomes our truth. The truth is that neither is true and both are true. We can be confident sometimes and not confident other times because we are just what we think and feel we are in each moment of our life.

If you can learn to be in a high level of universal consciousness, you will truly be in a place of no fear, no sadness, no anger, and no courage or lack of it. It is in this place of universal consciousness that a perfect state of well-being will be yours to enjoy.

You get to this place of mental health and well-being by becoming peaceful inside and then living in the present moment. In the present moment, you become highly aware of your surroundings. You think high-level thoughts, and then your universal mind is engaged with this energy. Sounds simple. It is simple when you get your inner thoughts set on being grateful and loving unconditionally.

You cannot fight and be angry when you are feeling love inside. You may not understand all that I say, but if you get that good feeling inside, you are "getting" the three principles. Live your life with a high level of consciousness present. To state it another way, live in the present moment, have a high degree of willingness to be aware of life around you, and be grateful for all you have. Be in the present moment, see what shows up, and then respond to that.

A movie is often used as an analogy to show the present moment with the principles in life. Here we see that the mind is the camera or the intelligence behind it all, the consciousness is the screen which makes you able to see the world or movie, and the movie being projected is the thought or the ideas ever flowing onto the screen or in your life. It's all just made up, but it sure seems real. That's our life.

CHAPTER 6

Thought

> "It is what we as humans put into our thoughts, that dictates what we think of our life. Thought on its own is a completely neutral gift."
>
> Quotation from *The Missing Link* by Sydney Banks

Thought can be described as the ideas that flow in and out of our mind. Thoughts are always passing through, and if there isn't a thought, well, wait a few seconds and there will be one. If you try to make yourself stop thinking of something, then you will surely think only about that. If I say, "Don't think about a black dog," then it is hard to tear yourself away from the thought of a black dog. It is the craziest damned thing how thoughts seem to work.

I believe that there are thoughts everywhere and they flow and have a negative or positive charge attached to them. We attract thoughts by the mood we are in and the vibration we are giving off. We learned earlier that emotions create a vibration, and now we see that the thought causes an emotion which creates a vibration.

So, it is back to the reality that energy and vibration are involved in everything. I will even go one step further to say that the thing that we think thinks is not the thing that thinks at all. To spell this out clearly, I do not think the brain is the great thinker in us. It took me a while to accept this idea that our brain may not be the only thinker in our life. All my life, I thought the brain was the only thinker. I learned to see the brain differently when I learned about the three principles.

Our brain is a mysterious organ that does a lot of things. It collects and stores all of our memories which can be brought to mind at will. It retains all of the information that we take in every day of our lives, as long as it is functioning properly. Our brains are quite remarkable, but I do not believe they are the main thinker and generator of fresh, new, insightful thoughts.

From both my understanding of brain functioning and my experiences with universal energy, I feel quite confident in saying that the brain does not do all of the thinking. Our brain sends signals to complex systems in our body and is the master of a lot of our day-to-day functioning. We start learning from the moment we are born, and the brain, like a sponge, holds all of that information. Like a massive computer, it can retain and regurgitate all that is stored in there.

However, the real generator of new thought is the universal mind. Einstein said something like, "It is not the intellect that gives new ideas, it is the imagination." The imagination is the universal mind.

It is the divine mind and consciousness that deliver the true gift of involution or new thought. The brain takes thoughts and then signals the body and our senses, which aid us in responding with an emotion. Following this emotion we will often have a behavioural response. If we interrupt this process and let the thought fall gently onto a peaceful mind, it is then that the new ideas and imagination can generate new insightful thoughts.

If you choose to stay with a thought, that is fine. Your free will allows you the choice of landing on the thought and staying with it or letting it go. The thoughts we stay on are the ones that create our life. If our thoughts create our life, wouldn't it be a good idea to really understand how to use our thoughts wisely?

It is really to our benefit to pay attention to our thoughts. Make those thoughts that you sit with and contemplate on the ones that will make your life better. Do not overthink things, as this is where you will get yourself into trouble. Mental illness is caused by thinking too much. Live with a quiet mind as much as you can.

When you are in a troubled place and trying to figure something out, don't go straight to thought. Silencing the mind will solve your problem much quicker and with a lot less stress. Some people are familiar with letting an unsolved problem sit for a while and not thinking about it, and then all of a sudden they intuitively know what to do. That is the universal mind sharing the knowledge that you are looking for.

You have probably experienced more of the principles than you realized, as we all just intuitively know things sometimes. We don't really know how we are able to just know these things sometimes. I will give you an example from my past. I was about to marry my first husband, and I knew this was not a good decision. Yet I convinced myself that I was in this situation and had to follow through with the plans. Even though my intuition told me it wasn't right, I went ahead with the marriage. We were divorced within a couple of years.

I should have listened to my intuition, which was divine mind speaking to me. We can ignore the truths that show up from our divine mind. Intuition is just a higher knowing of the universal mind. However, it is not usually to our benefit to ignore the intuition or the knowing that divine mind gives us.

We have all experienced the three principles through intuition. Realizing that you have already experienced the principles in action in your life makes it easier to understand them. Learning to understand your thinking is so important, and I have learned that intuition is usually a good thing to pay attention to. That inner knowing that you sense is quite a different thing than just the thoughts passing through.

When you intuitively know you should do or not do something, pay close attention to this, as it is usually the right thing for your future. But, as you can see from my example, I just changed the course when I knew I was not on the right path. I looked back at the intuition that had shown itself to me and said to myself, "You should have paid attention to that knowing." I learned a lot from the experience in that relationship, so all was not lost in my time spent there.

Don't spend too much time feeling you have made a mistake, as almost every learning experience will have a valuable lesson. From what I have learned from the principles, I would now just get quiet in the mind, ask what I should do in this situation, and the answer would show itself. I think the lesson to see here is that there are really no right and wrong decisions because we learn from all of the experiences.

So, don't sweat over decisions too much, as whatever decision you make will give experience to your life.

Direction taken can always be changed. Making decisions and paying attention to thoughts is all just on a learning curve. As you pay more attention to your thoughts, you begin to pay attention to the thoughts that are going to serve you well.

Learning to not pay too much attention to most of your thoughts is important, but don't take your thoughts too seriously. Most of your thoughts should pass on through your head. You may recall that most of our thoughts do not mean anything. Get comfortable with this reality.

Most thoughts have just floated in and should just float right out, not requiring your attention. I will often just shake my head and think, "Wow, where did that thought come from?" As you develop the ability to pay attention to your thoughts, you will then start to develop your higher level of thoughts and your higher level of consciousness. This will lead to a quieter mind and a closer connection to your universal mind. This is not only achievable for you, but it is also so easy when you just take it one step at a time.

CHAPTER 7

Science that Relates to Consciousness, Mind, and Thought

"All living creatures, great or small,
interpret what they think of life
via these three divine gifts."

Quotation from *The Missing Link*
by Sidney Banks, page 27

In studying evolution and simple organisms and complex species, we start to see developments that occur in the least complex organisms. These developments show that an understanding is occurring even when there is no brain present. I will show you my interpretation of a talk given by

Brendan Hughes, which can be found on YouTube. The talk, entitled "The Emergence of Universal Consciousness," suggests that our consciousness may be a part of the consciousness of the complex universal system. "Our being a part of the universal consciousness is how and why we adapt and adjust in our evolution of mind and body, which is energy in form, or mass, and formlessness or pure energy.

As the charged particles of energy combine and create mass, this leads to development of organisms and systems. The smallest particle, an electron, is a charged particle of energy. An atom is a component of electrons. Atoms combine to form molecules, and molecules combine to form organisms. Then organisms are components that develop into systems, such as ecosystems on planets. Planets make up solar systems which are components that become galaxies. These galaxies are components that form the universe. The universe makes up the whole, and its pieces are its parts.

So, each self is a part of the whole system or universe. You and I are just components in the larger self or whole system or universe. If an organism lived inside of you or me, then we would be its consciousness, and, being part of the system, the universe would be its larger consciousness.

If we look at the plant world, specifically the sunflower, we see that this plant follows and faces the sun. From morning until night its face turns to align with the sun. In fact, on cloudy days this plant just turns and faces the plant behind it, as there is no sun to follow. On these cloudy days, these plants appear to turn and share energy with one another. It would seem that they have a consciousness within themselves. It seems reasonable that they are a part of the whole and that they have the universal consciousness just by virtue of being a part of the whole and the universal energy flows in their form and formlessness.

The brain is a big software, like a big computer, that is powered by chemicals. This is also how neurology sees the brain. The brain is not a requirement for consciousness. If a living thing can be aware of and experience its environment, then it has and is a part of consciousness — like we saw with the sunflower.

Like the sunflower, bacteria signal each other and communicate. Being aware of and interacting with their environment means they have a consciousness. It would follow that the human they are in would be their bigger consciousness, and the bacteria would not be aware of the human's existence. The bacteria would only be aware of and interacting with the internal environment.

A specific bacterium named slime mould is unicellular and is titled Physarum Polyceiphalum. Though it is brainless, it exhibits a sort of spatial memory. As evidence of this, it avoids previously explored areas where it was not possible for it to multiply.

Bacteria have shown themselves to be an organized organism that evolves and changes and interacts with its environment; therefore, it follows that it has a consciousness. Humans and organisms evolve and have mutations or changes, and this brings about new possibilities. The universal consciousness has both involution and evolution occurring.

It has been suggested that the universe is expanding. Scientists have thought that it would expand to a point and then implode on itself. The newest theory is that the universe is expanding and will continue to expand, with no implosion expected. What if the universe is a part of yet a bigger system?

We know that scientists are only able to see some of the universe and that there are probably many solar systems. We do not know what is at the outer limits of the universe, but if there are outer limits, then we do know the universe is very large and it could very well be that the universe has an outer area that is a bigger system which it interacts with. Maybe there is another universe outside of this one? The thought of another universe outside of ours is so big that it is a bit nauseating to me; there is so much we don't yet know.

The universe consists of light energy and what science calls dark energy. We don't yet know what dark energy is or what it does, but we do know that approximately ninety per cent of the universe is made of this denser, dark energy. The light energy that we and planets are made of consists of about ten per cent of the universe. It is reasonable to say that we only know some things about the universe or energy that creates it all.

There is still a lot for science to learn, but it is quite reasonable and clear to me that the universe has a consciousness that holds all of the information of the past and the ideas of the future. Where there is consciousness, there is intelligence or mind and ideas or thought. So, the brain is not required to have mind, consciousness, and thought. If you have one of these principles, then you have all three as they always come together. Or, to say it another way, you cannot have one and not the other two.

Science and specifically quantum physics have come to realize that spirituality is a part of the essence of science and that you cannot have one without the other. Energy is the first element to exist, and it has an intelligence that allowed it to learn to combine in such a way to create mass. This is how the universe development moved along, and this is how we came to be humans in the form and formless energy.

CHAPTER 8

Finding your Wisdom

"The solution to outwardly complex problems created by misguided thoughts will not arise from complicated analytical theory, but will emerge as an insight, wrapped in a blanket of simplicity."

Quotation from *The Missing Link* by Sydney Banks

We often make our lives so complicated when the truth is that our lives could be so simple. When you have the three principles as a guide to live our life by, you can rid yourself of the difficulties that arise from anger, fear, and sadness. You will stop seeing yourself as broken and needing fixing.

It doesn't matter what situation you have come from or what situation you are going into; you are still whole and beautiful inside. Though we are all very different, we are also very much the same. Everyone just wants to be accepted and loved and to feel good about themselves, and this is possible and achievable.

It is my belief that you start the process of bringing the principles into your life by being grateful for what you have right now. You may be grateful for a friend you have, grateful for the sun shining today, or grateful for a roof over your head. Find the bright spots of good things in your life and be grateful for them.

Next, I want for you to be in the present moment in your life. We often miss good times in our life because we aren't present in the moment. If you are worrying about the past or worrying about the future, you will miss the present. Don't think about other things when you are conversing with others; listen to what they have to say. The art of listening to others is very important in your life. Keep your mind quiet as much as you can; most of our head chatter is not too helpful. When you sit quietly, watch for that comforting feeling inside; it is a gift every time you experience it.

Experience your life with a high level of consciousness by being aware of your thoughts and responding to them in ways that make you proud to be you. Always love yourself and others and show compassion for both them and you. Let your mind, intelligence, and intuition guide you. Have faith that you are always right where you are supposed to be in your life. Learn to speak to the universe with your words and your vibrations.

Put out to the universe all that you want in life, and I think you will be delighted to find that it all comes back to you. Laugh at yourself as much as you can; you are divine and probably often quite funny. Live your best life and don't accept any suggestion that you are broken; you are never broken. Love others unconditionally. Don't be afraid; you will always, always be okay. Your journey through life with the three principles will be very different than mine, but I know it can be great for you living on purpose with mind, consciousness, and thought to help you along the way. Live and love your life.

Your life now is important. Don't let memories of the past that are disturbing to you have a life in your present moment-to-moment living. Let the old troubling memories go by, realizing they have no power over you in the here and now. Our fear comes from the past troubling times.

We are all very afraid most of the time. We might be afraid of different things, but the foundation of fear is seen in our behaviours of anger, resentment, and sadness. If we choose to live without the fear, we then can truly live in kindness and love.

CHAPTER 9

The Self

"You must exercise your freedom of choice to decide on your own individual path."

Quotation from *The Missing Link*
by Sydney Banks, page 141

The self is ever-evolving, so changes are inevitable. Who you are today isn't necessarily who you will be tomorrow, so when we seek to find our self, well, that's easy, but it must be checked out daily as it is ever-changing. We are our beliefs, our judgments, and our thoughts. It seems to be more worth your while to let go of most beliefs and judgments and then just get curious about life. You will begin to see the possibilities and choices, and that's where you find out who you are.

I heard my four-year-old grandson say to himself, "Who am I?"

I asked him, "What did you just say?" and he repeated,

"Who am I?"

As he held his little forehead, I didn't know whether to laugh or cry for him. So I said to him, "Well, you are James; you are a wonderful, thoughtful, happy little boy who is loved very much by everyone around him."

Then he said, "But where did I come from?" I told him it was like his mama told him: he grew inside of her tummy and then when it was time, he was born. At that point our conversation was interrupted, and so we did not continue.

It would have been fun to see where that conversation might have gone; maybe someday we will do that. Wisdom flows through us whether we are young or old. I am guessing that he heard something on a T.V. show that led him to these thoughts. But, who knows: maybe he was having a little guy universal mind experience?

It's a good question, "Who am I?" I know I went on a search to try to find out who I was, in my twenties. Then I had a baby and those thoughts went on the back burner, with no time to return to them for quite a while. I think that when we ask this question about the self, we think that if we look outside of our self we will somehow find the answer. But it has become quite apparent to me that we need to look within to find this answer. So, we are back to going to our peaceful mind.

In our mind I think we are who we are told we are. This will change from day to day and situation to situation. From small children, like my grandson, we are told who we are by the way we are treated and by the way we begin to perceive ourselves in relation to others. If people tell us we never good enough then we start to believe this. Every time we try something new the thought arises of "I don't think I am good enough to play baseball or ride a bike." If we are told we are outspoken, then we act that way. I think our self evolves from others' perspective of us mostly, along with of course, our beliefs and thoughts. The exciting thing about this is we can change the belief and change the thought, so we can be anything we choose to be at any moment in time

It occurs to me that if we become who others think we are, then we can just as easily change this by becoming something other than that. I think we are all born with an essence of our individual self. We might be gentle, kind, or bold, for example. There are many different possible essences one can be born with. But, for the most part, we are just who we are taught to be. So you can go ahead and change who you are by having a new thought of who you are. Don't you love that?

Who we really are, our true self, is whoever we want that to be. We can change who we are whenever we want to do so. If you are lacking in confidence, know that is just what others have taught you to believe about yourself. Know that with a new thought, you can bring on a new self.

We never need to feel trapped into being who we believe we are because these are just assigned traits. Replace the trait that you don't want with the trait that you want. You never need to go on an outer journey to find yourself. You are always there inside yourself, and all is well. It is important to know that who you are from day to day, or minute to minute, can vary greatly. This is okay because different thoughts bring out different emotions, and this results in different behaviours. You don't ever have to be who others think you should be.

CHAPTER 10

Capabilities of the Mind

"There is no end or limitation, nor are there boundaries, to the human mind."

Quotation from *The Missing Link*
by Sydney Banks, page 35

We have looked at the universe, our mind, and our inner spiritual health in some detail. We know that our physical body reacts to our thoughts. For every thought that we have, there is an equal and reactive physical response in our body. For example, if you think to yourself, "My throat is sore. I bet I am getting sick; I seem to get sick so often lately. I am sure I am getting sick again," then you might feel the negative reaction you have created within yourself. You may just get sick the next day, and your thoughts may have contributed to this getting sick experience.

When I was six years old, my mom got very ill and she nearly died of spinal meningitis. Several years later, she told me that when she had meningitis, she could feel that she was dying and she had a conversation with God. She pleaded to be allowed to live and raise her children. My mom prayed to get well and told God that He could have her when her children were grown and had left home. She said that after her conversation and prayers, she immediately started to feel better, and she knew she would be okay; she would get healthy.

I really didn't think about that conversation much after that, as she was healthy and I had my mom back. Then, about seven years later, we all, my sisters and I, had grown and left home. It was five months after her last child left home that she died of cancer. Was this coincidence, or what had happened?

My understanding of this situation is that Mom, when she was sick, had, with a high vibration and frequency of energy, a conversation through universal mind with the divine universal energy or mind, and she made her desire very clearly known as to what she needed to happen. She then was literally healed by the universal energy with the positive belief that she had been granted her prayer to become healthy; her vibration and frequency of love were heard and brought to life. It was a miracle, and yes, miracles happen. Her personal energy and that of the universal energy combined forces, and anything is possible when that happens. She did indeed get to raise her children.

Then, when her children were grown and had left home, she believed she would become ill and die. This was on her mind a lot in the few years prior to her death. And, indeed, this is what occurred. It may have been the case that if she had again asked the divine power to let her live, she could have lived much longer. I don't know. Maybe, maybe not. What do you think?

It would have been wonderful to have had her with us longer. She was such a loving, giving, spirited person. I do know that her spirit lives on even today, and it is a great source of comfort for me to know this. Her beautiful spirit lives on, in and around me. Mom, in form, is gone. She left her physical body, but her spirit or pure energy lives on forever. I believe it was her destined time for her to leave life on Earth.

When a loved one dies, you can take comfort in knowing that their spirit lives on. You don't need to fear your own death either, as your spirit will also live on. You can live your life with no fear of the end coming. There is no end to you or me. Our self in form will end, but our formless spirit will live on forever.

I think that the other important lesson to learn here is that we can ask the divine universal energy for whatever we need. When asking for what you need, have good intentions and loving emotions. This leads to a high vibration and the universe will hear you. Ask for it, see it, and feel it as if it is already here, and then you will receive it. You are a divine being made of form and formless energy; embrace this and your life will be wonderful.

Get to know your magnificent mind by being loving and grateful for what you have, and then get quiet inside and your inner wisdom, your mind, will surface and answer any question you may have. We are much more powerful than most of us realize.

When you gain an understanding of the power of your mind, you realize that you can make whatever you want happen in your life. It is true that our emotions cause us to have a vibration at certain frequencies. If you are feeling anger or hate, you emit a vibration at the lowest frequency. However, if you are feeling loving feelings, then you have a vibration at the highest level or frequency. We are always emitting these vibrations and attracting that frequency which we are vibrating at. So, when people talk about raising the vibration of the planet, this is actually just one person at a time feeling loving feelings. When enough people emit the frequency of high vibrations, this can and will raise the vibration of the planet.

CHAPTER 11

Love

"Love is not just an idea. Love is a living, breathing essence that the wise can pluck from the air at will and then like a master artist mold it into something beautiful. Love makes the impossible, possible."

Quotation from *Second Chance*
by Sydney Banks, page 86

I think love is what can keep us all sane and connected, but it can also make us crazy and unconnected. The choice is really yours. If you put too many qualifiers on your love, then the love becomes a burden. What I mean by that is if you think, "I will love you as long as you make me happy," then you have put an external expectation on this love, and your partner now has to act in ways that keep you happy. I don't think this is love; instead, I think this is self-sabotage. It is an unreal expectation for someone, other than yourself, to make you happy.

Once you can make you happy, then you can find a healthy love that isn't dependent on the other person being a certain way. After all, we should all be allowed to be ourselves and act in ways that align with who we really are. I also think that who we really are changes every day, so love must be flexible. I would like to see what love is not, and then, with those things placed aside, see what is left that is love.

Jealousy is not love. Love is also not present when one is physically or verbally abusing another. There is no love present when one is judging, belittling, or attaching in a suffocating manner to the other. Love is not present when a person does not take the time to stop and look to see what the other person looks like and feels like and what another has to say about anything and everything. The list seems long of what love is not. So, what is love?

It is my belief that love is a feeling, not an emotion. Love, in its truest formlessness, has some real freedom that comes along with this feeling. Love that comes from the spirit or the formless energy is not subject to the whole male-female way of thinking. Instead, love is purely the exquisite feeling that starts in the stomach and very softly grows with warmth and gratitude. It shows in your eyes and is present in your words. Love leaves you feeling grateful and joyful. When you live in the present moment, it is possible to feel love for everyone that crosses your path.

When people are with you, and you are present in that moment, it is possible to feel kind and compassionate toward them and this is also part of love. If you are kind and compassionate and place no conditions or judgment in that moment, then you feel the warm, soft, gentle feeling in your stomach. That's love. It seems to me that there are many different interpretations of what love is and is not.

Love is kindness, love is being patient with one another, and love is caring about how the other person feels. These three ways of being encompass a lot of what love is. Love also comes with no judgment. I think that the purest love can only come from those who love themselves.

The more you love yourself, the more you can love others. When someone says, "Have love for all," what does that mean? I think it means that when you learn to love yourself, then you can feel love for all others, and you can feel however much love you choose to feel for the other person. You can literally turn the frequency or vibration up or down.

It is very reassuring to know that you can choose just how much you are going to love someone. That's cool, because then you don't have to fear this love that we are speaking of. You are free to feel love or not feel love from the formless part of your spirit or energy. In the form, things get a bit more complicated if you put a lot of thought into this.

In form or mass, our energy comes from either a feminine or a masculine perspective, and this will definitely bring the ego into play. It is from this place that love becomes complicated or not complicated. This too is your choice of how you bring the feeling of love into the emotions of form.

In the form, we get all of these contradicting and confusing pieces of the puzzle of love. If, for example, you are holding on so tight to the other person that they feel they have no space in the relationship, well, this is not really love. This is really insecurity and fear of loss, which is not a very blissful mixture of emotions to attach to the feeling of love.

Simply stated, if you want happiness for the other person, accept them for who they are, and then let in the feeling of love. You will be loving from the formless energy and spirit. Watch for and try to minimize the complicating ego ideas.

It is easy to see the ego states of judgment, jealousy, and insecurity try to enter your state of being. Minimize these thoughts and love from the purest formless energy. This is where the curiosity of life and the magic of the universe rest, always ready for you to awaken to this state of love.

To awaken to your pure love in formlessness, put most thoughts aside and feel the feeling. Then watch as so many of your fears fall away and life becomes a joyful experience. Oh yes, and don't forget to not take yourself too seriously, because we make it all up one thought at a time. Except for love, pure love is the real goal in life to learn and live with. Love is really all that matters.

ACKNOWLEDGEMENTS

I would like to thank the following people for their help on this journey of writing this book. Each person has touched my life in profound and different ways. Love to all of you.

Dr. Bill Pettit, for sharing his wisdom and mentoring me; I so much enjoyed our talks.

Dr. Linda Pettit, for her support and help in understanding important issues; I loved our talks as well.

Michael Neill, for his work in the form of books and courses to help us all understand our inner world better.

Scott Allan, for sharing his knowledge and skills necessary to write a book, for his coaching, and for his encouragement.

Michele Johnson, as my accountability partner helping me to keep on track with consistent writing.

Chandler Bolt, for designing such a comprehensive program, The SPS, to guide me through, step by step, how to get my book from my head onto paper.

DeLynn Steele Cooley, for talking through some of our shared difficulties in accomplishing this task of book-writing.

Tellwell staff editors and artists and project manager, for helping me take my book to the next level. Your technical skills have been so appreciated.

Marnix Pauwels, for hours of talking and seeing me through getting a deeper understanding of me in this whole new world I have awakened to seeing and living in. I would recommend his coaching to almost everyone, as he seems to effortlessly awaken people to a much richer experience of life.

Rae, Jessie, and Kerri, my family, for your love and support.

My email address, should you wish to contact me with questions, is:

jchristenson7387@gmail.com

The Non-Profit organization started in 2020 can be reached at: https://insearchofapeacefulmind.ca here you will find coaching for corporate managers and employees, as well as coaching for individuals and free coaching for the homeless is available at this time.

WORKS CITED

Banks, Sydney. *Second Chance*. Lone Pine Publishing, 1987.

Banks, Sydney. *The Enlightened Gardener*. Lone Pine Publishing, 1987.

Banks, Sydney. *The Missing Link*. Lone Pine Publishing, 1998.

Holmes, Ernest. *The Science of Mind*. General Press. 1988.

Hughes, Brandon. "Consciousness." *YouTube*, uploaded March 2019.

Neill, Michael. *The Inside-Out Revolution*. Hay House Inc., 2013.

Printed in Great Britain
by Amazon